How to Draw
CROCODILES
and Other Reptiles

Peter Gray

PowerKiDS
press™

Published in 2014 by The Rosen Publishing Group, Inc.
29 East 21st Street, New York, NY 10010

Illustrations: © Peter Gray
Editors: Joe Harris and Nicola Barber
U.S. Editor: Joshua Shadowens
Design: sprout.uk.com
Cover design: sprout.uk.com

Library of Congress Cataloging-in-Publication Data

Gray, Peter, 1969
 How to draw crocodiles and other reptiles / by Peter Gray.
    pages cm. — (How to draw animals)
 Includes index.
 ISBN 978-1-4777-1301-3 (library binding) — ISBN 978-1-4777-1413-3 (pbk.) —ISBN 978-1-4777
1414-0 (6-pack)
 1. Reptiles in art. 2. Crocodiles in art. 3. Drawing—Technique. I. Title.
 NC783.8.R45G73 2014
 743.6'79—dc23

2012047586

Printed in China
SL002687US

CPSIA Compliance Information: Batch #AS3102PK: For Further Information contact Rosen
Publishing, New York, New York at 1-800-237-9932

CONTENTS

THE BASICS

DRAWING

The first stages of a drawing take you from the basic outlines of your picture to adding shade and texture.

Build up the general shape of your subject with guidelines.

Guidelines

I have drawn the guidelines quite heavily to make them easy to follow, but you should work faintly with a hard pencil.

Detail

Use a softer pencil to develop the character and details. You may find that you do not follow the guidelines exactly in places. That's fine—they are only a rough guide.

Shading and texture

Carefully erase the guidelines and mistakes. Then add shading and texture with a soft pencil.

INKING

For a bold look, go over the outlines with ink. Wait for the ink to dry thoroughly, then erase all the pencil marks.

Felt-tip pen outlines

The easiest inking method is to use a felt-tip pen. If you plan to add paint at a later stage, make sure your pen is waterproof or the paint will run.

Brush outlines

For a more graceful effect, use a fine-tipped **watercolor** brush dipped in ink.

COLORING

Although I use watercolors in this book, the main principles are the same for any materials—start with the shading, then add in markings and textures, and finally, work your main colors over the top.

Felt-tip coloring

Felt-tip pens produce bright, vibrant colors. Work quickly so that the pen strokes do not remain visible.

Colored pencils

Colored pencils are the easiest coloring tools to use, but you have to take great care to blend the colors to achieve a good finish.

Watercolors

The subtlest effects can be achieved with watercolor paints. It is best to buy watercolor paints as a set of solid blocks that you wet with a brush. Mix the colors on a palette or on an old white plate.

SCALES

Different creatures have different types of scales. Following these steps will help you to get them right.

The way you use the guidelines depends on the effect you are after.

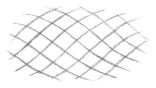

Tortoise **Crocodile** **Snake**

The tortoise's rough scales follow the guidelines very loosely.

The more even scales of crocodiles are bold and regular.

The smooth scales of snakeskin are very precise and fine.

COLORING

Both coloring and highlights help to capture the feel of an animal's skin texture.

Tortoise

The tortoise's scales are dull in color with deep shading.

Crocodile

Snake

Snakes and lizards tend to be smoother, which you can show with bright **highlights**.

QUICK SCALES

When you draw a whole creature, don't try to fill in every scale.

These examples are less detailed but still capture the effect of the different scales.

Tortoise **Crocodile** **Snake**

CLAWS

Reptiles have distinctive feet and claws, which can sometimes be awkward to draw. Some careful guidelines can really help.

TORTOISE FEET

The tortoise has solid, chunky feet with big claws that are more like toenails.

Sketch in the main foot first. Add curves to mark the upper and lower positions of the claws.

Draw in evenly spaced lines to position the claws around the foot.

Now you can use your guidelines to create the tortoise's claws.

CROCODILE FEET

A crocodile's feet are a little bit like human hands.

Draw the shape of the palm and then a curve that marks the length of the fingers.

Add pointed shapes spreading outward for the fingers.

Flesh out the fingers, add webbing in between, and draw the short claws at the tips.

IGUANA FEET

The feet of the iguana are complicated, with fingers of different lengths.

Draw a palm shape, then mark the rough positions and lengths of the fingers.

Mark the joints as circles along the length of the finger lines.

Flesh out the fingers, then draw the claws on the ends.

CROCODILE

The biggest and heaviest of all living reptiles, the crocodile is a fearsome hunter. It has powerful jaws and sharp teeth for grabbing prey. The scales on the underside of the crocodile are small and smooth. On its back, it has large, ridged scales that act as protective armor.

1 Start with a long, smooth curve that runs all the way around the crocodile's powerful tail and body. Then add a neat circle in front as a guide for the crocodile's unusual neck shape.

2 Add the jaws and the beginnings of the legs. Now the crocodile starts to take shape.

3 Connect the head, neck, and body with a few lines, and add eyebrow ridges. Then sketch in the feet—five toes on the front feet, four on the back. Start to map out the ridges on the back, drawing the outer edges and the center line.

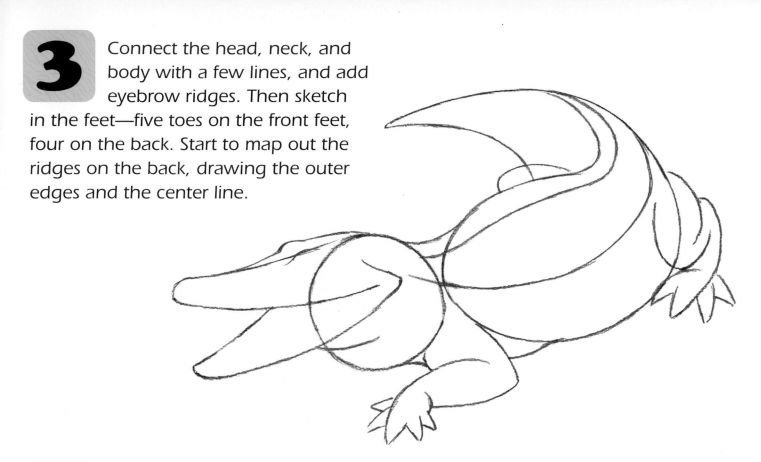

4 Now flesh out the details— the lines of the mouth and teeth, the claws and webbed toes. Fill in the guidelines for the back ridges. They should be evenly spaced on the body, but they should get smaller along the tail.

5 This is where the fun starts! Now that the guidelines are all in place, you can sketch the details with your pencil, refining and reshaping the drawing wherever necessary. You can erase the guidelines as you go.

6 For this example, I did most of the inking with a brush. I also used a fine felt-tip pen for the delicate details of the teeth. For the shadow and texture of the crocodile's underside, I used crisscross shading to follow the curve of the rounded body.

7 The first stage of painting is the shading. Decide on a direction for the light to come from—here, it is upper right. Mix up a **neutral** gray color. Try to avoid using black paint—it's much better to mix a gray from other colors, for instance, purple with a little brown and blue.

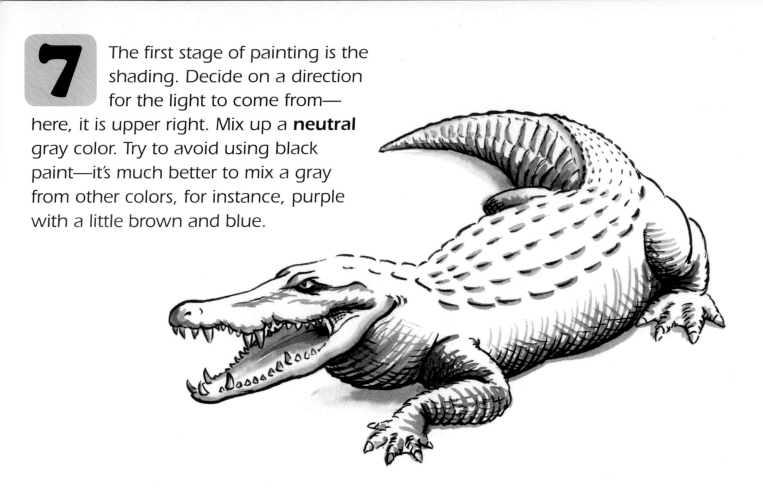

STEALTH CROC

A swimming crocodile can be hard to spot in rivers and lakes. The only parts that remain visible above the surface of the water are the crocodile's nostrils, eyes, and ears, which are on the highest part of its head. The rest of the crocodile's massive body is hidden beneath the surface.

ANIMAL FACTS

8 For the crocodile's markings, I mixed up a dark gray-green (again using no black paint) and painted broad, rough stripes down the back. I used the tip of the brush for more delicate dabs and spots.

9 Paint flat colors over the top of the shading and markings. This will blend all the paintwork together, softening the edges. I used two colors, mid-green for the back and yellow-brown for the undersides. Make sure the paint is not too thick or dark, or the layers underneath will not show through.

10 Now it's time to add tiny spots of color for highlights, on the eyes and claws, for example. Look hard at your picture to see if any areas need brightening. For highlights, you will need some white paint or ink, or you could use a sharpened piece of chalk. The highlights bring out the shine on a subject and show up its texture.

COBRA

The cobra is a deadly snake that attacks either by biting or by spitting venom into the eyes of its prey. When threatened, the cobra rears up and spreads its neck ribs to form a distinctive "hood" shape. The king cobra is the world's largest poisonous snake—it can grow to over 16 feet (5 meters) in length.

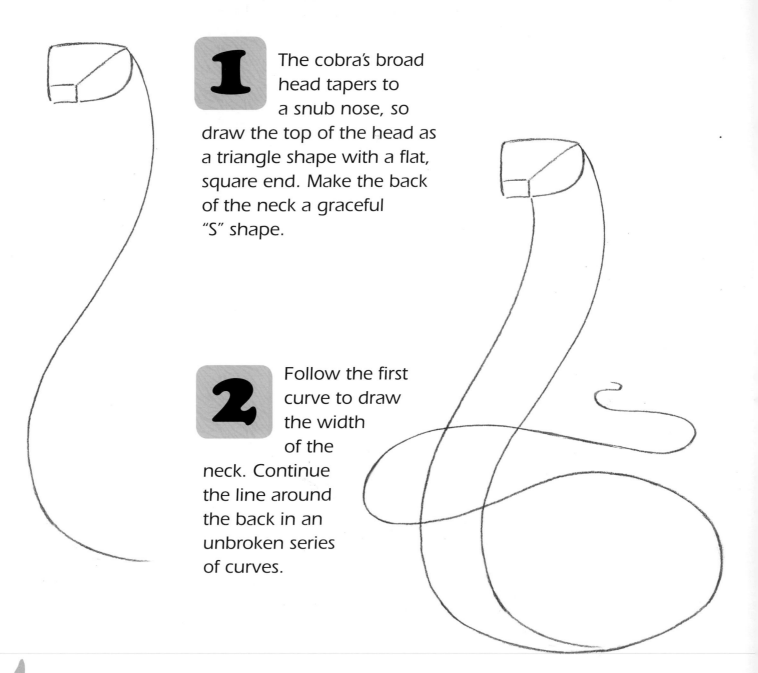

1 The cobra's broad head tapers to a snub nose, so draw the top of the head as a triangle shape with a flat, square end. Make the back of the neck a graceful "S" shape.

2 Follow the first curve to draw the width of the neck. Continue the line around the back in an unbroken series of curves.

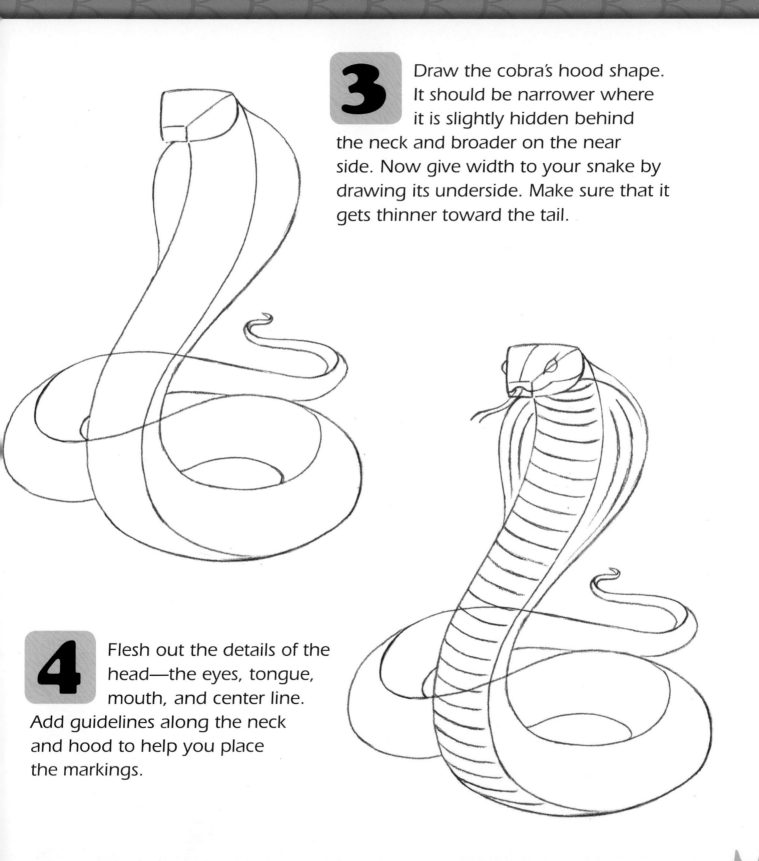

3 Draw the cobra's hood shape. It should be narrower where it is slightly hidden behind the neck and broader on the near side. Now give width to your snake by drawing its underside. Make sure that it gets thinner toward the tail.

4 Flesh out the details of the head—the eyes, tongue, mouth, and center line. Add guidelines along the neck and hood to help you place the markings.

SPITTING SNAKE

When cobras bite, they inject venom (poison) through two fangs at the front of the mouth. But some cobras have an extra defense. Spitting cobras spray venom from their fangs. The snake targets the attacker's eyes—although it is harmless on skin, the venom quickly starts to cause blindness.

ANIMAL FACTS

5 Develop the face and markings with more pencil work. It may look a bit scruffy, but you can clean it up after the next stage.

6 Ink in the outline and the markings. Notice how the ink line is much heavier around the outline than it is for the markings and details.

7 Cobras come in many different colors and patterns. I've chosen yellow and black—nature's warning colors! I added a touch of scaly texture to the body at this stage but not too much, because I didn't want to distract attention from the head and the hood.

IGUANA

The iguana is a large lizard that lives in Central America and the Caribbean. Male iguanas can grow to up to 6 feet (2 meters) in length. The iguana uses its sharp eyes to look for food. If it is attacked, it lashes out with its long, whiplike tail.

1 Draw a long egg shape for the iguana's body, then the outer edge of the tail flowing smoothly on from its back. The head should be drawn separately and is roughly triangular in form.

2 Now join the head and body with curving lines to make the iguana's shape. The tail should get narrower toward the tip. Start to work on the legs by carefully marking the outer edges.

3 Iguanas have strange feet, so spend some time getting them right. For now, the toes can be simple lines. You can also draw a branch for the iguana to sit on.

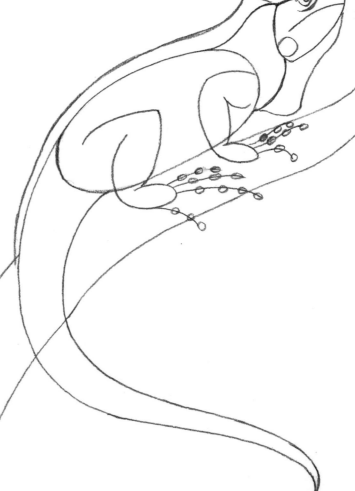

4 A line down the back will be your guide for the iguana's spikes. Add more detail to the head. To help with the complicated knuckles in the feet, draw small circles on each of the joints.

5 Now you can add the finishing touches to your pencils. Follow the guidelines drawn in stage 4 as you add detail to the feet.

6 Use a thin brush or a fine pen for the delicate lines of the spikes, claws, and fingers. You can ink more heavily in some of the shadow areas and add texture to the branch.

TAIL TRICKS

If an attacker grabs hold of an iguana's tail, the iguana has a cunning trick. It allows its tail to drop off. The iguana then runs away! In time, a perfect new tail will grow in its place.

ANIMAL FACTS

7 For creatures of more than one color, try to blend the colors into each other. This effect is tricky with felt-tips but is fairly easy with colored pencils. If you are using paint, you should work the two colors together while they are wet.

GIANT TORTOISE

Giant tortoises are ancient creatures that can grow to a huge size. Their bodies are protected by thick, domed shells. They eat plants and can survive for long periods of time without food and water, living off the stores of fat in their own bodies.

1 Start with a neat arch. Be careful as you add the other curves—they will form the shape of the shell.

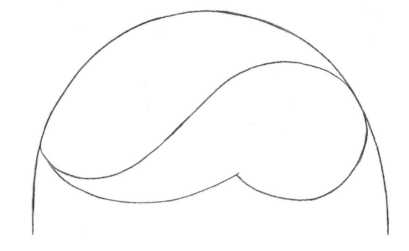

2 The legs begin with simple ovals. The neck is simple, too, but the head ends in quite a sharp angle for the tortoise's nose shape.

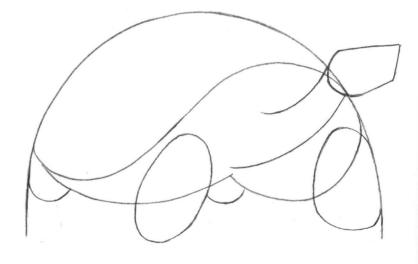

3 Adding the feet and face is straightforward, but take care with the edge of the shell. It is easy to make it look lopsided if you're not careful.

4 Fill in more detail on the shell, then sketch the toes. Now you will have all the guidelines you need to develop the drawing in pencil.

5 For the detailed pencil stage, the main areas to work on are the face, neck, and toes. It's also a good idea to add some texture to guide the inking. Decide on the direction of light, and draw most of the texture in the areas of shade.

6 You don't need to outline everything in ink. I have allowed the line to fade out around the top of the shell for a lighter feel. This will make a good contrast with the heavily textured legs and neck. The neck should look really wrinkly.

OLD AGE

Giant tortoises can live for a very long time. In the wild, many giant tortoises survive well beyond their hundredth birthdays. In zoos, they often live even longer. One giant tortoise is thought to have reached the amazing age of 255!

ANIMAL FACTS

7 The tortoise is mostly plain gray and brown all over. I have slightly varied the colors of the body and shell to make them more interesting. I have used dull highlights because this creature is not very shiny.

JUNGLE SCENE

Now that you have mastered drawing individual reptiles, it's time to experiment with putting them into a natural scene.

1 The first stage of developing a scene is a rough pencil drawing on scrap paper. This is to figure out the sizes and positions of all the elements in the scene. Don't worry if you make lots of changes and do lots of erasing before you are happy with the result.

2 Before moving on to a more detailed artwork on good paper, you can plan your colors and shading by quickly coloring in your rough drawing. The idea of a color rough is to find out what does and doesn't work before you start on the final artwork.

3 To complete the color rough, I have used a black felt-tip to define the outlines and deep shadows, as well as some white ink for highlights. I also decided to add some more **foliage** in the foreground and to darken some of the shading in the background and river.

4 On a fresh sheet of good paper, draw guidelines for the main shapes that make up the picture. Work across the whole surface without getting into details. Think of the plants as broad shapes.

5 Gradually build up the detail. Use the skills you have learned in this book to develop the animals, then work on the surrounding elements. Draw in the details of the foreground plants, but make those in the background more sketchy. You can still make changes—I decided to alter the plants in the foreground from those in my color rough.

6 Use a sharp pencil to refine the whole drawing. Pay attention to the characters of the animals. Try to keep the individual shapes of the plants clearly defined. Erase any confusing marks and guidelines.

7 It is a good idea to start inking in the elements that are closest to the front of the picture, then work backward. Use strong, confident strokes to make the plants and leaves graceful. Marks in the background should be finer and less distinct.

8 Start with the shading in a neutral color, as you did with the crocodile on page 11. Vary the colors of green for the different plant types. I have used brighter colors around the iguana and duller colors near the crocodile.

GLOSSARY

foliage (FOH-lee-ij) A general term for plants and leaves.

guidelines (gyd-LYNZ) In a drawing, light lines to indicate where a finished line should go.

highlights (HY-lyts) Bright areas in a painting or drawing.

neutral (NOO-trul) In painting, a neutral color is one such as gray or beige that matches well with most other colors.

texture (TEKS-chur) The appearance and feel of a surface.

watercolor (WAH-ter-kuh-ler) Paint made from pigment (color) that dissolves in water.

WEBSITES

Due to the changing nature of Internet links, PowerKids Press has developed an online list of websites related to the subject of this book. This site is updated regularly. Please use this link to access the list:

www.powerkidslinks.com/HTDA/rept

FURTHER READING

Ames, Lee J. *Draw 50 Animals.* New York: Watson-Guptill, 2012.

McCarthy, Colin. *DK Eyewitness Books: Reptile.* New York: Dorling Kindersley, 2012.

McCurry, Kristen. *How to Draw Incredible Dinosaurs.* Mankato, MN: Capstone Press, 2012.

INDEX